SO-BAK-333

E____ G. BESSEY SCHOOL
LIBRARY
SCARBOROUGH   MAINE

the true book of

TROPICAL FISHES

By Ray Broekel

Tropical fishes are an absorbing hobby whether you have just two guppies in a bowl or set up and maintain a well-balanced twenty-gallon aquarium.

It is no secret that a child will read eagerly along his own interests.

Here, for beginners, is a book packed with simple, well-organized, constructive information about the kinds and needs of fresh-water tropical fishes.

The text, simple enough for a young reader, is interpreted and extended with many colorful pictures.

Ray Broekel is a general science teacher and author of a monthly column for the Aquaria Department of a national magazine.

The "true book" series is prepared
under the direction of
Illa Podendorf
Laboratory School, University of Chicago
Ninety-eight per cent of the text is in words from
the Combined Word List for Primary Reading

ELWOOD G. BESSEY SCHOOL
LIBRARY
SCARBOROUGH   MAINE

the true book of
TROPICAL FISHES

BY RAY BROEKEL
Illustrated by Rocco Dante Navigato

CHILDRENS PRESS, CHICAGO

GUPPY

ZEBRA

Copyright, 1956, Childrens Press
Printed in the U.S.A.

5 6 7 8 9 10 11 12 13 14 15 16 17 18 19 20 21 22 23 24 25   R   75 74 73 72 71 70 69

CONTENTS

ZEBRA

TROPICAL CATFISH

Tropical fishes live where it is warm.
Most of them live in countries near
the equator.

The weather near the equator is
almost always warm.

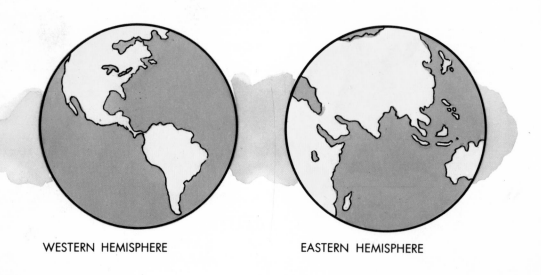

WESTERN HEMISPHERE   EASTERN HEMISPHERE

Some live in the oceans and are called
salt-water tropicals.

Some live in lakes, rivers, streams, and ponds. These are the fresh-water tropical fishes. This book is about fresh-water tropical fishes.

Most tropical fishes live in the countries that are in Central America, South America, Asia, and Africa.

Tropical fishes are caught by people who live there.

Sometimes people who sell tropical fishes take trips to collect them.

Then the fishes are taken to sea-ports,

or airports.

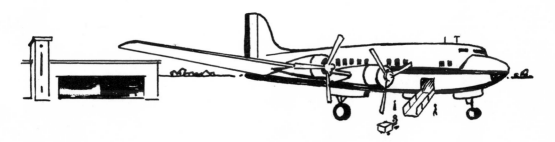

Then they are shipped or flown to the United States or other places in the world.

In the United States, trains,

trucks,

and airplanes

take them to all parts of the country.

Finally they reach your pet store.

Lots of tropical fishes are also raised in our country by tropical-fish dealers.

Some tropical fishes have babies that are born alive.

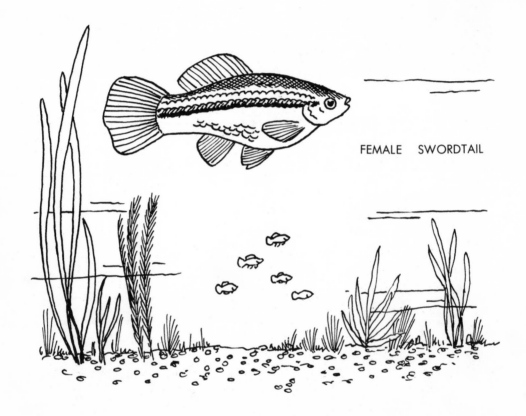

FEMALE   SWORDTAIL

Tropical fishes that have their babies born alive are called live-bearers.

Some tropical fishes have babies
that are hatched from eggs.

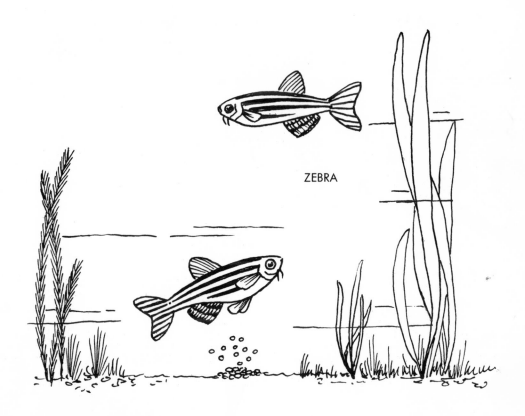

ZEBRA

Tropical fishes that have babies
that are hatched from eggs are
called egg-layers.

The guppy is a popular tropical fish.

MALE GUPPY

FEMALE GUPPY

RDN

Guppies are easy to take care of.
They do not bother other fishes.
Grown-up guppies are about one inch long.
Baby guppies are born alive.
Guppies are live-bearing tropical fishes.

The angel fish looks like a black-
striped silver dollar floating in
the water.

ANGEL FISH

Baby angel fishes hatch out of eggs.
Angel fishes are egg-laying tropical
fishes. Grown-up angel fishes are about
the size of a silver dollar.

There are many kinds of catfishes.
Tropical catfishes mainly come
from the countries in South America.

TROPICAL CATFISHES

Catfishes are scavengers. Scavengers
eat things that many other fishes do
not eat.

It takes some food a very short time to spoil in water. Most tropical fishes will not eat food after it is spoiled.

Catfishes, however, do eat spoiled food. That is why they make good aquarium fishes.

They help keep the aquarium clean.

Catfishes will not bother other fishes.

Baby catfishes hatch from eggs.

Siamese fighting fishes are bubble-nest builders. The male Siamese fighting fish blows bubbles from his mouth to cover the eggs.

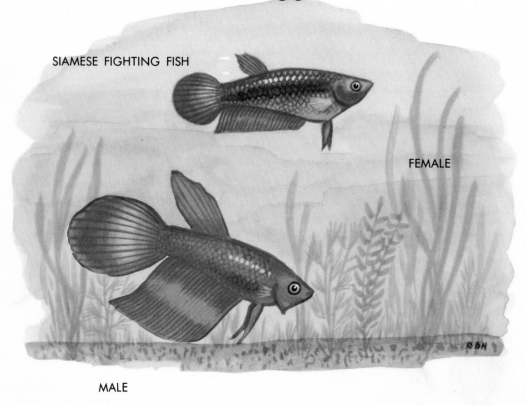

SIAMESE FIGHTING FISH

FEMALE

MALE

The male watches the eggs until they hatch out.

Siamese fighting fishes have long, wavy fins. Male Siamese fighting fishes will fight with each other.

MALE SIAMESE FIGHTING FISH

You should never keep more than one male Siamese fighting fish in an aquarium.

Zebra fishes never seem to rest. They move about very quickly. They are striped somewhat like a real zebra.

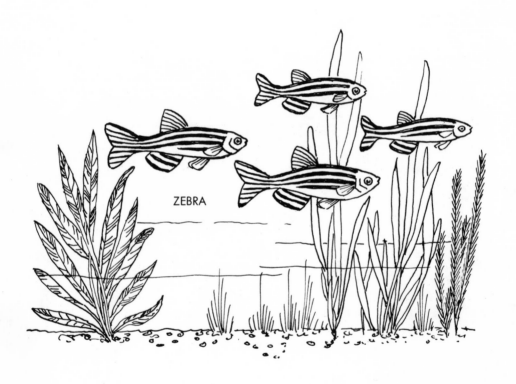

ZEBRA

That is why they are called zebra fishes. Zebra fishes are egg-layers.

Swordtails are strange-looking
tropical fishes. A part of their
tail fin looks like a sword. Only
the male swordtails have these swords.

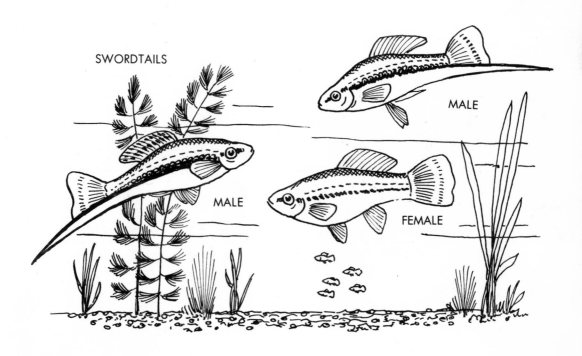

SWORDTAILS

MALE

MALE

FEMALE

Swordtails are live-bearers.
Baby swordtails are born alive.

Neon tetras are colored a bright, shiny red and blue.

Neon tetras are among the most beautiful of the tropical fishes.

NEON TETRAS

Grown-up neon tetras are very small. They are much smaller than guppies. Baby neon tetras hatch from eggs.

You can tell how bloodfins got
their name by looking at the picture.

BLOODFINS

Bloodfins move about quickly in
the water.
They are a peaceful fish.
Bloodfins are egg-layers.

Platy fishes are also called moons.
There are many different kinds of
platys.

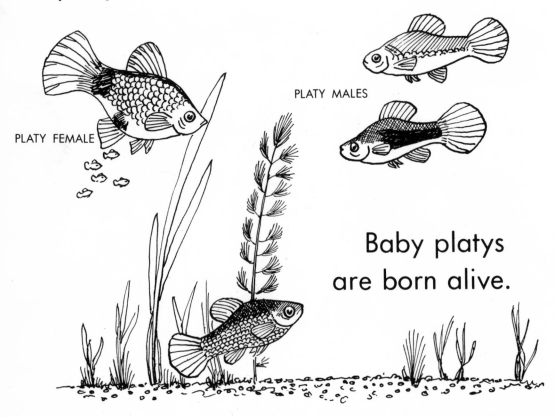

PLATY MALES

PLATY FEMALE

Baby platys
are born alive.

Platys are nice tropical fishes to
have in an aquarium.
They do not fight with other fishes.

SNAILS AND PLANTS FOR AN AQUARIUM

Snails, like catfishes, are scavengers.

RAMSHORN
SNAIL

Snails help eat
left-over food.

AFRICAN SNAIL

Most snails
lay eggs.

Snails are
interesting
to watch.

POND SNAIL

MYSTERY SNAIL

Snails move about
very slowly.

Plants that live in water, like plants in a garden, need light to help them grow.

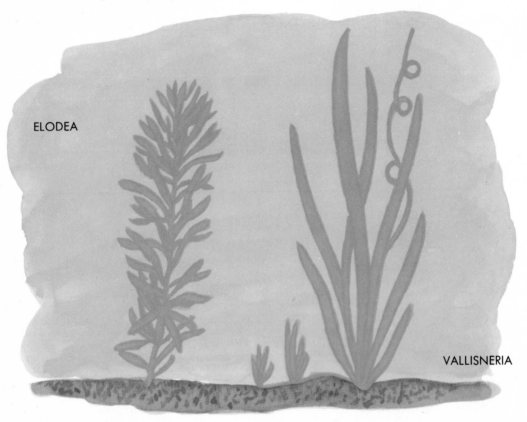

ELODEA

VALLISNERIA

Plants, when they have light, give off a gas called oxygen.

Fishes need oxygen.

Most water plants have roots that

SAGITTARIA

HYGROPHILA

grow down into the gravel or sand.
Some water plants float in the water.
The roots of these plants float in
the water.

WATER FERN
(top view)

AMAZON SWORD
PLANT

Water plants grow and die just
as plants in the garden do.
They are green when they are alive.
They turn brown when they are dead.

28

MYRIOPHYLLUM

CABOMBA

CRYPTOCORYNE
WILLISII

YOUR AQUARIUM

Do not put your aquarium where it will get too much sunlight.

ALGAE SEEN THROUGH
A MICROSCOPE

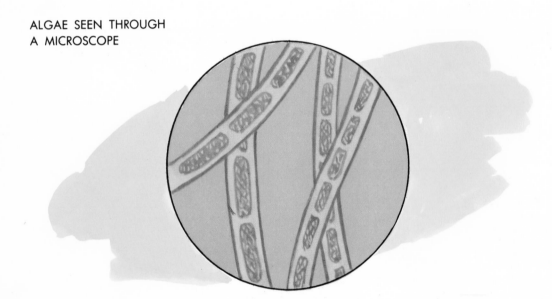

If you do, tiny plants called algae will start growing.

Place your aquarium in a spot where the plants will get enough light to stay green.

A reflector will give off enough light to keep your water plants green. It also helps to keep the water warmer.

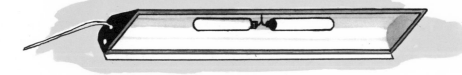

REFLECTOR SHOWING LIGHT BULB

GETTING YOUR AQUARIUM READY

Use about two pounds of aquarium gravel for each gallon of water.

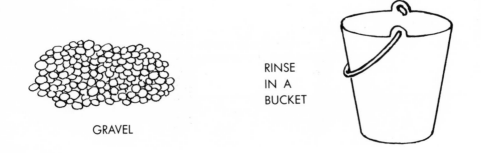

GRAVEL

RINSE
IN A
BUCKET

Wash the gravel carefully.
Fill the aquarium half full of water.

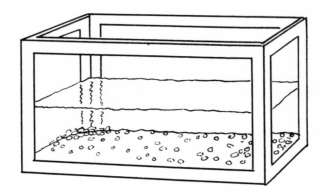

Now put in your plants.

Then carefully fill the aquarium
to the top with water.

Pour the water in slowly over your
hand, so it will not stir up the sand.

Let your aquarium plants grow for
at least one week before you put in
any fishes.

Always let water you are going to use in your aquarium sit for at least twenty-four hours in a glass jar or an enamel pan.

This will let the chlorine gas rise out.

Chlorine gas is deadly to fishes.

Chlorine gas is put into water to kill the germs.

This makes it safe for us to drink.

Chlorine is added to water at the city pumping or filtering stations.

Check the temperature of the water
with an aquarium thermometer. Make
sure the temperature
is around 72 degrees.

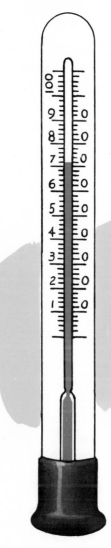

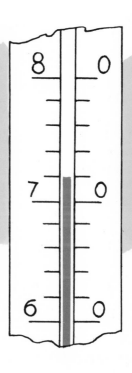

Don't put too many fishes into your aquarium. Give them lots of room so that they can grow into healthy fishes.

OVER-CROWDED FISH

HEALTHY FISH

If your fishes are always at the top of the aquarium, you might have too many fishes in it.

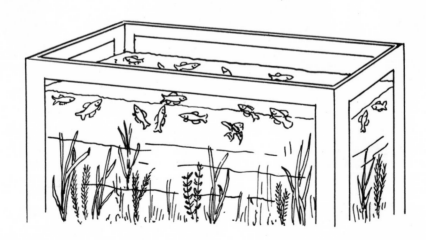

Feed your fishes a little food two or three times a day. The food that would cover this spot O is about enough for three fishes for one meal.

Too much food can cause your gravel to turn black. Then the water will smell bad.

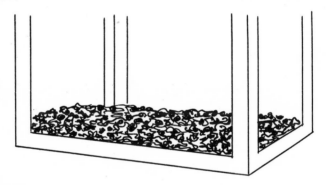

You will then have to clean your aquarium and start all over again.

Fishes can go without food for days. So, if you forget to feed them once in a while, it will not harm them.

Aquariums come in many sizes. The larger the aquarium, the more fishes you can keep.

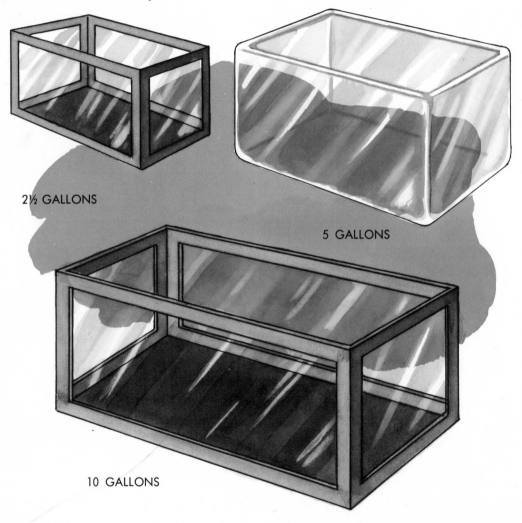

2½ GALLONS

5 GALLONS

10 GALLONS

SOME THINGS YOU WILL NEED

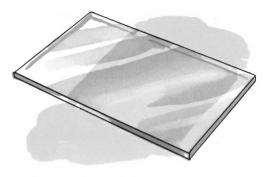

A piece of glass to place on top of your aquarium will help keep dust out.

Nets are handy when you need to catch some of your fishes.

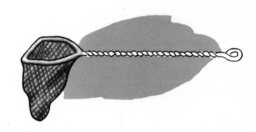

A little tropical fish food will last for a long time.

OTHER THINGS YOU CAN USE

An air pump will
help put more oxygen
into the water and
to clean the water.

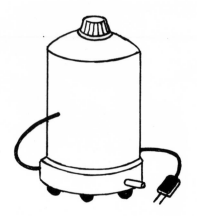

The air pump forces
air through plastic
tubing.

The tubing runs into
a valve.

The knob on top of the
valve can be turned.

By turning the valve knob you
allow the air to go
into the air stone,

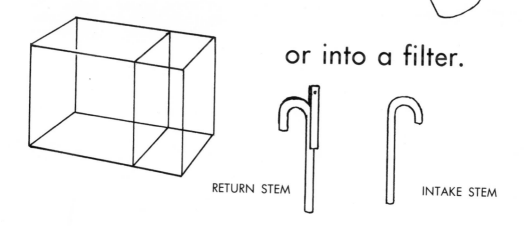

or into a filter.

RETURN STEM

INTAKE STEM

Charcoal in the filter
cleans the dirt out of
the water. The clean
water then goes back
into your aquarium.

41

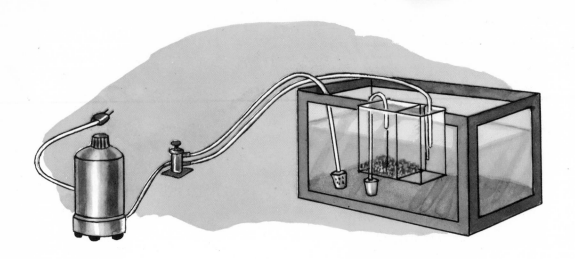

A pump, valve, filter, air stone, and plastic tubing are shown all hooked together.

A rubber hose to siphon dirt off the bottom of your aquarium is useful.

Reflectors are very handy because the light bulb inside the reflector gives off light. This light helps your plants grow. Algae usually will not grow under reflector light.

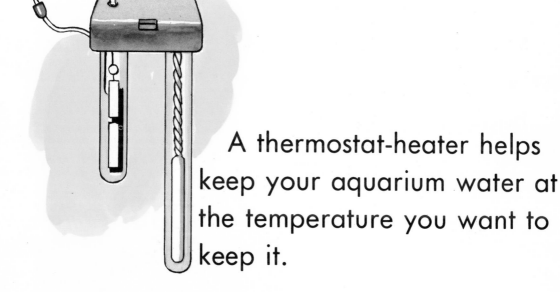

A thermostat-heater helps keep your aquarium water at the temperature you want to keep it.

A little control knob is at the top. You turn this knob to get the temperature you want.

IMPORTANT THINGS TO REMEMBER

Don't feed too much food.

Don't let the temperature of the water go below seventy degrees. Your fishes might get sick if you do.

Don't try to keep too many fishes in one aquarium.

Your tropical fishes must have plenty of room to be healthy.

Don't tap or rap on the aquarium glass. This scares the fishes.

TWICE AROUND

THE CLOCK

Make sure to let water stand for at least twenty-four hours before putting it into the aquarium.

Chlorine gas is deadly to tropical fishes.

Fishes breathe oxygen gas and give off carbon dioxide gas, just as human beings do.

GILL

We breathe through our noses.
Fishes take in water through their mouths. Oxygen is taken from the water into the gills of the fish.
Then the oxygen is passed into the body of the fish.
The carbon dioxide in the water then goes back into the water from the gills.

A clean aquarium with healthy plants makes a wonderful home for tropical fishes.